I0450425

WETLAND STATUS AND TRENDS
FOR THE HACKENSACK MEADOWLANDS

An Assessment Report from
the U.S. Fish and Wildlife Service's National Wetlands Inventory Program

by

Ralph W. Tiner, John Q. Swords, and Bobbi Jo McClain

U.S. Fish and Wildlife Service
National Wetlands Inventory Program

U.S. Fish and Wildlife Service
Northeast Region
300 Westgate Center Drive
Hadley, MA 01035

December 2002

This report should be cited as: Tiner, R.W., J.Q. Swords, and B.J. McClain. 2002. Wetland Status and Trends for the Hackensack Meadowlands. An Assessment Report from the U.S. Fish and Wildlife Service's National Wetlands Inventory Program. U.S. Fish and Wildlife Service, Northeast Region, Hadley, MA. 29 pp.

Table of Contents

Introduction

The Hackensack Meadowlands is perhaps the largest urban wetland complex in the northeastern United States. It lies along the Hackensack River and is located within the New York-Newark metropolitan area. Given this location, the Meadowlands has been greatly impacted by urban and port development.

The New Jersey Field Office of the U.S. Fish and Wildlife Service (Service) has been working in the Meadowlands and elsewhere to improve conservation and restoration of wetlands. This Office requested that the Service's National Wetlands Inventory (NWI) Program conduct a wetland trends analysis to document recent changes in wetlands in the Meadowlands area. Since the 1970s, the NWI Program has been producing wetland maps across the country and conducting assessments of wetland trends for the Nation as well as for local areas (visit websites: wetlands.fws.gov and northeast fws.gov/wetlands for additional information about NWI). In the spring of 2002, the Northeast Region's NWI Program received strategic mapping funds from the Service's Washington Office to perform an analysis of wetland change for the Hackensack Meadowlands using remote sensing techniques.

Purpose of Report

The main purpose of this report is to document how wetlands in the Meadowlands area changed from the 1950s to the 1990s. The emphasis is on quantitative changes (i.e., changes in extent; acreage) and not on qualitative changes in wetlands. The report also presents other information that provides a valuable perspective on these and prior changes.

Study Area

The Hackensack Meadowlands is located in Hudson and Bergen counties in northeastern New Jersey. The study area includes the Meadowlands (the Hackensack Meadowlands District) and wetlands along the north bank of the Passaic River from Newark Bay and the confluence of the Passaic River and the Hackensack River, north to an area just above its confluence with Overpeck Creek (Figure 1). The study area is slightly larger than the officially designated Hackensack Meadowlands District. It includes all or portions of the following communities: Kearny, Jersey City, Secaucus, Union City, North Bergen, Fairview, Ridgefield, Ridgefield Park, Little Ferry, Moonachie, South Hackensack, Hackensack, Teterboro, East Rutherford, Rutherford, Carlstadt, Woodridge, Hasbrouck Heights, Lyndhurst, North Arlington, and Harrison. This area is dominated by tidal wetlands and the lower Hackensack River. The Hackensack Meadowlands has been identified as significant habitat complex in the New York/New Jersey Harbor Area (U.S. Fish and Wildlife Service 1996).

Figure 1. Location of the study area in the New York City-Newark metropolitan area.

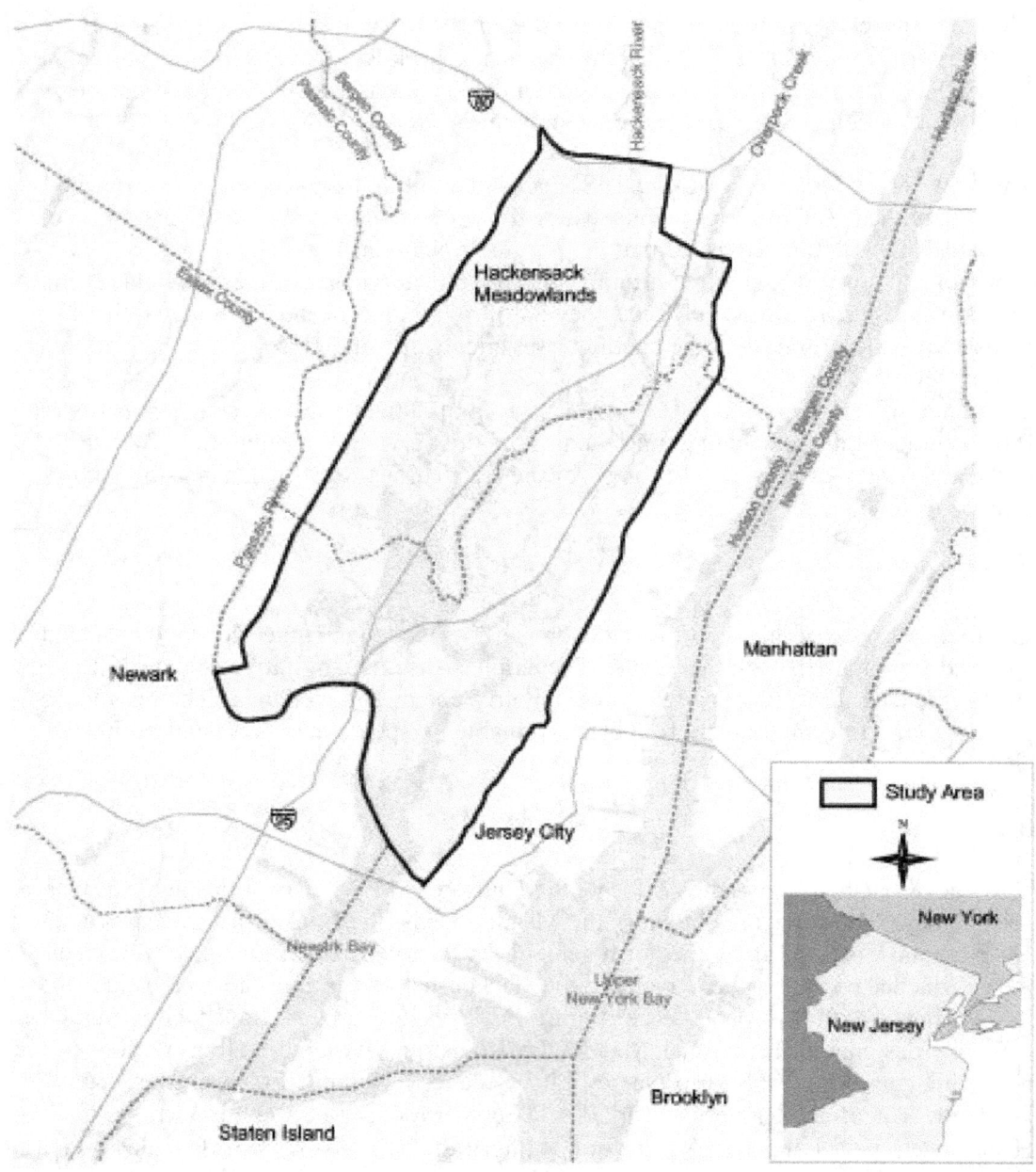

Methods

The Service is updating NWI maps for much of northern New Jersey by interpreting 1995 aerial photography. These maps and the accompanying digital data are compiled by taking the State of New Jersey's digital 1986 wetland data (posted on the web at http://www.state.nj.us/dep/gis/wetshp.html), reclassifying wetlands consistent with regional NWI techniques, and updating these data based on interpretations of 1995 1:40,000 color infrared photography (acquired by the U.S. Geological Survey's National Aerial Photography Program). Updating is accomplished by using a digital transfer scope (DTS) to superimpose digital wetland data on the 1995 aerial photos. Edits to the digital data are made through geographic information system (GIS) technology (i.e., ArcView software at http://www.esri.com) that is incorporated into the DTS system. Wetlands are classified according to the U.S. Fish and Wildlife Service's official wetland classification system (Cowardin et al. 1979), and limited field checking is performed. From these digital data for Hudson and Bergen counties, we created a digital wetland database for the Meadowlands study area.

Conventional photointerpretation techniques were employed to identify and record wetland changes in the Meadowlands since the 1950s. Table 1 outlines the aerial photography used for this study. The study examined, in detail, wetland changes from the 1950s to the 1960s, the 1960s to the 1980s, and the 1980s to the 1990s. General assessments of wetland trends from 1966 to 1976 and from 1976 to 1984/85 were performed by comparing newly acquired data from this study with the original NWI data (1976 1:80,000 black and white photography). Detailed analysis was not performed due to the small-scale of this photography. It was used to fill a gap between the 1960s and 1980s data to provide a perspective on wetland losses midway between these dates. In addition, a historical topographic map from 1889 was used to prepare a map showing the distribution and extent of wetlands during the late 19th Century. The map was obtained through the New Jersey Environmental Digital Library housed at Rutgers University and posted on the web at http://njedl.rutgers.edu/njdlib/.

After creating the 1990s wetlands database, we then compared the 1980s imagery with the 1990s photos (using the DTS) to detect and record the nature of the change in wetlands (e.g., loss to residential development or gain from estuarine open water) and deepwater habitats. Areas (polygons) of change were delineated and labeled to the cause of change. The Anderson et al. (1976) classification system was used to categorize changes in land use and/or upland cover. After the 1990s-1980s analysis was performed, the 1980s-1960s change detection was done, followed by the 1960s-1950s analysis. This "reverse trends analysis" procedure produced a digital database with a few hundred polygons that had changed at one time or another during the study period.

Table 1. Aerial photography used for detailed examination of wetland trends in the
Meadowlands area.

Month/Year	Scale	Emulsion
March 1995	1:40,000	Color Infrared
March 1984/85	1:58,000	Color Infrared
February 1966	1:24,000	Black and White
June 1953/February 1954	1:20,000	Black and White

A series of figures or maps were produced to show the changes in wetland distribution
and extent in the Meadowlands region over time. Although 1970s photography was not
used in our comprehensive analysis of wetland trends, the Service had produced original
NWI maps for New Jersey in the late 1970s/early 1980s using 1:80,000 black and white
photography. The digital data for these maps were used to generate a 1976 snapshot of
Meadowlands wetlands. Some edits were made to these data based on interpretations of
more detailed aerial photos from the 1980s and 1960s. The end result is that we were
able to produce a time series of maps that showed changes in wetland extent on a 10-year
cycle from the mid-1950s to the mid-1990s.

From an 1889 topographic map of Bergen, Hudson, and Essex Counties (Figure 2), we
interpreted the extent of wetlands based on marsh/swamp symbols. By merging these
data with our 1950s-era wetland data, we were able to prepare a figure and accompanying
statistics (wetland and deepwater habitat acreage) showing Meadowlands wetlands in the
late 19th Century. This product provided an interesting perspective on wetland losses
predating recent times. These data were compared with the results of our detailed
analyses to reveal wetland and deepwater habitat trends since the late 1800s.

Figure 2. A portion of the 1889 topographic map for Bergen, Hudson, and Essex counties showing the Hackensack Meadowlands study area (outlined in red). (Source: http://njedl rutgers.edu/njdlib/)

Results

Recent Trends in Wetlands and Deepwater Habitats

Since the trends analysis was derived through photointerpretation of aerial photos, the results represent an approximation of wetland changes over time. This study represents the most detailed examination of recent wetland changes in the Meadowlands region performed to date. Wetland trends were examined in detail for three periods: 1) mid-1950s to mid-1960s, 2) mid-1960s to mid-1980s, 3) mid-1980s to mid-1990s. A comparison of wetland trends from 1889 to 1995 (including a general assessment of trends from 1889 to the mid-1950s, the mid-1960s to the mid-1970s, and the mid-1970s to the mid-1980s) is given in the last section of the Results.

1950s to 1960s

In the 1950s, the Meadowlands region possessed over 13,400 acres of wetlands (Table 2) and nearly 2,850 acres of deepwater habitats (2,806.9 acres - estuarine; 7.5 acres - lacustrine; 32.4 acres - riverine). Estuarine vegetated wetlands represented almost 90 percent of the wetlands. Emergent wetlands dominated or co-dominated by common reed (Phragmites australis) were most abundant. This plant is an invasive species that readily colonizes disturbed soils and wetlands, especially coastal wetlands where tidal flow is restricted or where fill has been deposited.

From 1953/4 to 1966, over 2,760 acres of vegetated wetlands were converted to upland or ponds (Table 3). Only 6.8 acres of wetlands were created, for a net loss of 2,756 acres. The gains were 6.8 acres of palustrine tidal emergent wetlands coming from cleared upland (5.4 from sand/gravel land and 1.4 from transitional land). Twenty-one percent of the 1950s estuarine vegetated wetlands was destroyed. Thirty-eight percent of the loss was attributed to fill with an unidentified use (transitional land[1]), 36 percent was due to conversion of vegetated wetlands to estuarine water (presumably by dredging operations), and 15 percent to industrial development.

Pond acreage also experienced a net loss of 14 acres (Table 4). Most of the losses were attributed to transitional land (unknown use) and transportation/communication facilities.

Deepwater habitats gained over 1,000 acres (net gain of 1,008.3 acres) during this decade. Nearly 1,000 acres of estuarine deepwater habitat came from estuarine emergent wetland (Table 3). Construction of a 25.7-acre impoundment (lacustrine) on cleared upland (transitional land) also added to the deepwater habitat acreage. Loss of deepwater habitat was limited to just 13.1 acres (7.5 acres of lacustrine habitat were filled for unknown use and 5.6 acres of estuarine water were converted to mostly urban land).

---

[1] Most (56%) of the transitional land identified from 1966 to 1995 became industrial land by 1995, while 15% became transportation/communication facilities, 10% other urban built-up land, 7% institutional/governmental land, 5% residential, 4% transitional land (in 1995), 2% shrub rangeland, and 1% commercial development land.

Table 2. Extent of wetlands in the Meadowlands region in 1953/54.

Wetland Type	Acreage
Estuarine Wetlands	
Aquatic Bed Regularly Flooded	1.0
Emergent Irregularly Flooded	11,773.7
	(includes 11,159.4 a. w/Phragmites)
Emergent Regularly Flooded	167.9 (includes 87.0 a. w/Phragmites)
Scrub-Shrub Irregularly Flooded	13.0
Emergent/Scrub-Shrub Irregularly Flooded	22.8 (includes 18.6 a. w/Phragmites)
Scrub-Shrub/Emergent Irregularly Flooded	10.7 (includes 2.3 a. w/Phragmites)
--	--------------------
Subtotal Estuarine Vegetated	11,989.1
Unconsolidated Shore Regularly Flooded	462.9
Unconsolidated Shore Irregularly Flooded	3.4
--	--------------------
Subtotal Estuarine Nonvegetated	466.3
Total Estuarine	12,455.4
Palustrine Wetlands	
Emergent Tidal	236.1 (includes 171.4 a. w/Phragmites)
Emergent Nontidal	224.2 (includes 56.0 a. w/Phragmites)
Scrub-Shrub Tidal	17.2
Scrub-Shrub Nontidal	22.0
Emergent/Scrub-Shrub Tidal	57.2 (includes 22.6 a. w/Phragmites)
Emergent/Scrub-Shrub Nontidal	24.4
Forested Tidal	103.1
Forested Nontidal	65.5
Scrub-Shrub/Forested Tidal	16.1
Scrub-Shrub/Forested Nontidal	66.7
Forested/Scrub-Shrub Nontidal	11.3
--	--------------------
Subtotal Palustrine Vegetated	843.8
Unconsolidated Bottom Tidal	21.1
Unconsolidated Bottom Nontidal	64.0
Unconsolidated Shore Tidal	10.7
Unconsolidated Shore Nontidal	16.5
--	--------------------
Subtotal Palustrine Nonvegetated	112.3
Total Palustrine	956.1
Riverine Wetlands	7.5
GRAND TOTAL – ALL WETLANDS	13,419.0

Table 3. Extent and causes of vegetated wetland loss from 1953/54 to 1966.

Wetland Type	Cause of Loss	Acres Lost
Estuarine Emergent	Residential Development	58.9
	Commercial Development	46.5
	Industrial Development	363.8
	Transportation/ Communication	57.4
	Other Urban Land	95.2
	Filled Unidentified Use	949.9
	Converted to Estuarine Water	995.7
	Pond Creation	6.6
	Subtotal	2,574.0
Estuarine Emergent/Shrub	Residential Development	0.8
	Industrial Development	0.9
	Subtotal	1.7
Estuarine Shrub/Emergent	Filled Unidentified Use	8.4
Palustrine Emergent Tidal	Industrial Development	10.9
	Transportation/Communication	8.8
	Filled Unidentified Use	43.3
	Pond Creation	0.2
	Subtotal	63.2
Palustrine Emergent Nontidal	Commercial Development	3.0
	Industrial Development	8.6
	Transportation/Communication	5.4
	Other Urban Land	0.5
	Agriculture	3.6
	Filled Unidentified Use	7.6
	Pond Creation	1.5
	Subtotal	30.2
Palustrine Emergent/Shrub Tidal	Filled Unidentified Use	34.7
Palustrine Forested Tidal	Residential Development	5.5
	Industrial Development	20.0
	Filled Unidentified Use	13.3
	Pond Creation	0.1
	Subtotal	38.9
Palustrine Forested/Shrub Nontidal	Transportation/Communication	1.8
	Other Urban Land	9.5
	Subtotal	11.3
Total Vegetated Wetland Loss	All Causes	2,762.4

Table 4. Extent and causes of changes in pond acreage from 1953/54 to 1966.

Cause of Change	Acreage Gain from	Acreage Loss to	Net Change in Acreage
Residential Development	-	1.4	-1.4
Commercial Development	-	0.9	-0.9
Industrial Development	0.7	4.7	-4.0
Transportation/Communication	-	5.6	-5.6
Transitional Land (unknown use)	-	10.3	-10.3
Excavated Estuarine Emergent Wetland	6.5	-	+6.5
Excavated Tidal Fresh Wetland	0.3	-	+0.3
Excavated Nontidal Emergent Wetland	1.5	-	+1.5
Totals	9.0	22.9	-13.9

1960s to 1980s

At the start of this period (1966), the Meadowlands region possessed 10,650 acres of wetlands (Table 5) and about 3,855 acres of deepwater habitats (3,797.1 acres - estuarine; 25.7 acres - lacustrine; 32.4 acres - riverine). Estuarine vegetated wetlands of common reed predominated.

From 1966 to 1984/85, nearly 4,870 acres of vegetated wetlands were converted to upland or waterbodies (Table 6). Industrial development was responsible for about one-third of the losses. Filling with unidentified use (development not yet built) was the second-leading cause of vegetated wetland loss, with about one-fourth of the loss attributed to this activity. Other significant causes of vegetated wetland loss were recreational development (including the Meadowlands Sports Complex; 12% of the losses), transportation/communication facilities (11%), and dredging of estuarine emergent wetlands (10%). Most of the vegetated wetland losses affected estuarine wetlands. Half of the 1966 acreage of these salt and brackish marshes was destroyed (i.e., converted to dryland or water) during the following two decades.

Besides the vegetated wetland losses, 66.7 acres of estuarine unconsolidated shore (tidal flats) were filled to create developable land. The use of most of this acreage (62.3 acres) was undetermined (i.e., land in transition), while the rest was converted to recreational land (3.6 acres), ponds (0.4 acres), and industrial development (0.4 acres).

Only 38.6 acres of wetlands (excluding ponds) were created from the mid-1960s to the mid-1980s, for a net loss of 4,907 wetland acres for the Meadowlands region. All the gains came from cleared upland, except for 0.2 acres of estuarine emergent wetland created from estuarine water. The gains from upland were 4.6 acres of estuarine emergent wetlands (4.4 acres from upland with unidentified use and 0.2 from estuarine water) and 34.0 acres of palustrine vegetated wetlands (31.7 acres of tidal emergent; 1.5 acres of nontidal emergent; 0.8 acres of tidal forested).

Pond acreage experienced a slight net gain of 8 acres (Table 7). A total of 44.3 acres was created, while 36.3 acres were converted to upland. The gains came mostly from former vegetated wetlands (43.0 acres from excavation of mostly former estuarine emergent wetlands), while a 1.3-acre pond was built on cleared upland.

Human activities during this time period appear to have produced a significant gain in deepwater habitat. A net gain of 465.5 acres resulted from a 485.0-acre gain and a 19.5-acre loss. Nearly all of this gain was attributed to an increase in estuarine deepwater habitat acreage at the expense of tidal marshes. Dredging of these marshes was identified as the cause for 471.3 acres of newly created estuarine water, while 0.3 acres of estuarine water were created by excavating upland. An additional 13.4 acres came from impoundment construction on cleared upland (transitional land). During this period, 19.3 acres of estuarine water were converted to dryland for urban uses including transportation and industrial facilities, while 0.2 acres of estuarine water became estuarine emergent wetland.

Table 5. Extent of wetlands in the Meadowlands region in 1966.

Wetland Type	Acreage
Estuarine Wetlands	
Aquatic Bed Regularly Flooded	1.0
Emergent Irregularly Flooded	9,199.7
	(includes 8,947.1 a. w/Phragmites)
Emergent Regularly Flooded	167.9 (includes 87.0 a. w/Phragmites)
Scrub-Shrub Irregularly Flooded	13.0
Emergent/Scrub-Shrub Irregularly Flooded	21.1 (includes 18.6 a. w/Phragmites)
Scrub-Shrub/Emergent Irregularly Flooded	2.3 (includes 2.3 a. w/Phragmites)
---	--------------------
Subtotal Estuarine Vegetated	9,405.0
Unconsolidated Shore Regularly Flooded	462.9
Unconsolidated Shore Irregularly Flooded	3.4
---	--------------------
Subtotal Estuarine Nonvegetated	466.3
Total Estuarine	9,871.3
Palustrine Wetlands	
Emergent Tidal	174.5 (includes 133.7 a. w/Phragmites)
Emergent Nontidal	194.0 (includes 52.3 a. w/Phragmites)
Scrub-Shrub Tidal	17.2
Scrub-Shrub Nontidal	22.0
Emergent/Scrub-Shrub Tidal	28.0 (all. w/Phragmites)
Emergent/Scrub-Shrub Nontidal	24.4
Forested Tidal	64.4
Forested Nontidal	65.5
Scrub-Shrub/Forested Tidal	16.1
Scrub-Shrub/Forested Nontidal	66.7
---	--------------------
Subtotal Palustrine Vegetated	672.8
Unconsolidated Bottom Tidal	22.8
Unconsolidated Bottom Nontidal	52.8
Unconsolidated Shore Tidal	10.7
Unconsolidated Shore Nontidal	12.1
---	--------------------
Subtotal Palustrine Nonvegetated	98.4
Total Palustrine	771.2
Riverine Wetlands	7.5
GRAND TOTAL – ALL WETLANDS	10,650.0

Table 6. Extent and causes of vegetated wetland loss from 1966 to 1984/85.

Wetland Type	Cause of Loss	Acres Lost
Estuarine Emergent	Residential Development	85.5
	Commercial Development	233.7
	Industrial Development	1,530.2
	Transportation/ Communication	484.4
	Other Urban Land	88.0
	Recreational Land	560.9
	Shrub Rangeland	17.5
	Filled Unidentified Use	1,194.9
	Converted to Estuarine Water	471.3
	Pond Creation	24.6
	---	---------
	Subtotal	4,691.0
Estuarine Emergent/Shrub	Industrial Development	2.5
	Filled Unidentified Use	6.4
	---	--------
	Subtotal	8.9
Palustrine Emergent Tidal	Industrial Development	10.0
	Transportation/Communication	13.3
	Pond Creation	1.0
	---	--------
	Subtotal	24.3
Palustrine Emergent Nontidal	Residential Development	0.8
	Commercial Development	0.6
	Industrial Development	25.2
	Transportation/Communication	12.4
	Other Urban Land	52.1
	Shrub Rangeland	2.6
	Filled Unidentified Use	3.0
	Pond Creation	4.6
	---	---------
	Subtotal	101.3
Palustrine Emergent/Shrub Tidal	Other Urban Land	24.4
Palustrine Forested Tidal	Transportation/Communication	13.7
	Other Urban Land	3.4
	Recreational Land	1.0
	---	--------
	Subtotal	18.1
Palustrine Forested Nontidal	Industrial Development	2.5
Palustrine Scrub-Shrub Nontidal	Other Urban Land	4.7
	Filled Unidentifed Use	3.7
	---	---------
	Subtotal	8.4
Total Vegetated Wetland Loss	All Causes	4,878.9

Table 7. Extent and causes of changes in pond acreage from 1966 to 1984/85.

Cause of Change	Acreage Gain from	Acreage Loss to	Net Change in Acreage
Industrial Development	-	15.1	-15.1
Transportation/Communication	-	4.9	-4.9
Other Urban Built-up Land	-	3.6	-3.6
Transitional Land (unknown use)	1.3	2.3	-1.0
Recreational Land	-	8.8	-8.8
Shrub Rangeland	-	1.6	-1.6
Excavated Estuarine Emergent Wetland	37.0	-	+37.0
Excavated Estuarine Unconsolidated Shore	0.4	-	+0.4
Excavated Tidal Fresh Wetland	1.0	-	+1.0
Excavated Nontidal Emergent Wetland	4.6	-	+4.6
---	------	------	------
Totals	44.3	36.3	+8.0

1980s to 1990s

In the 1980s, the Meadowlands region had about 5,738 acres of wetlands (Table 8) and nearly 4,321 acres of deepwater habitats (4,249.3 acres - estuarine; 39.1 acres - lacustrine; 32.4 acres - riverine). Estuarine emergent wetlands colonized by common reed were the predominant wetland type.

From 1984/85 to 1995, 182.2 acres of estuarine emergent wetlands were converted to upland and 22.5 acres were dredged to create estuarine deepwater habitat for a total loss of nearly 205 acres.[2] The causes of vegetated wetland loss are summarized in Table 9. Besides the vegetated wetland losses, 0.3 acres of estuarine unconsolidated shore (tidal flats) were filled to create developable land. Only 2.6 acres of vegetated wetlands were created (i.e., palustrine emergent wetland from upland), for a net loss of 202.1 acres. Four percent of the 1980s acreage of estuarine vegetated wetlands was eliminated during this decade.

Pond acreage experienced a slight net gain of 5.1 acres due to the construction of seven small nontidal ponds on upland. No losses of ponds were detected during this period.

A small net gain of 15.2 acres in deepwater habitat took place during this decade. Twenty-eight acres of estuarine water were created (5.5 acres from upland and 22.5 acres from tidal marsh). A total of 12.8 acres of estuarine water was filled for roads and other development in progress at the time (unidentified use).

---

[2] The difference between the extent of estuarine emergent wetland from 1984/85 to 1995 (204.6 acres) and the change of 204.7 acres of loss listed in Table 9 is due to round-off.

Table 8. Extent of wetlands in the Meadowlands region in 1984/85.

Wetland Type	Acreage
Estuarine Wetlands	
Aquatic Bed Regularly Flooded	1.0
Emergent Irregularly Flooded	4,564.8 (includes 4,441.3 a. w/Phragmites)
Emergent Regularly Flooded	103.8 (includes 87.0 a. w/Phragmites)
Scrub-Shrub Irregularly Flooded	13.0
Emergent/Scrub-Shrub Irregularly Flooded	12.2 (all w/Phragmites)
Scrub-Shrub/Emergent Irregularly Flooded	2.3 (all w/Phragmites)
Subtotal Estuarine Vegetated	4,697.1
Unconsolidated Shore Regularly Flooded	396.2
Unconsolidated Shore Irregularly Flooded	3.4
Subtotal Estuarine Nonvegetated	399.6
Total Estuarine	5,096.7
Palustrine Wetlands	
Emergent Tidal	181.9 (includes 164.6 a. w/Phragmites)
Emergent Nontidal	94.2 (includes 27.0 a. w/Phragmites)
Scrub-Shrub Tidal	17.2
Scrub-Shrub Nontidal	13.6
Emergent/Scrub-Shrub Tidal	28.0 (all w/Phragmites)
Forested Tidal	47.1
Forested Nontidal	63.0
Scrub-Shrub/Forested Tidal	16.1
Scrub-Shrub/Forested Nontidal	66.7
Subtotal Palustrine Vegetated	527.8
Unconsolidated Bottom Tidal	34.5
Unconsolidated Bottom Nontidal	48.9
Unconsolidated Shore Tidal	23.1
Subtotal Palustrine Nonvegetated	106.5
Total Palustrine	634.3
Riverine Wetlands	7.5
GRAND TOTAL – ALL WETLANDS	5,738.5

Table 9. Extent and causes of estuarine wetland loss from 1984/85 to 1995.

Wetland Type	Cause of Loss	Acres Lost
Emergent	Commercial Development	2.1
	Industrial Development	26.9
	Transportation/Communication	16.3
	Other Urban Land	5.5
	Recreational Land	28.6
	Shrub Rangeland	28.7
	Filled Unidentified Use	74.1
	Converted to Estuarine Water	22.5
	--	---------
	Subtotal	204.7
Unconsolidated Shore	Filled Unidentified Use	0.3
Total Wetland Loss	All Causes	205.0

Status of Wetlands and Deepwater Habitats in the 1990s

In 1995, about 5,541 acres of wetlands were inventoried in the Meadowlands region (Figure 3). Wetlands occupied over 1000 acres more than deepwater habitats which totaled 4,336 acres.

Wetlands

Estuarine wetlands were most abundant, representing 88 percent of the area's wetlands (Table 10). The remaining wetlands were palustrine types, with the exception of just 7.5 acres of riverine wetlands (seasonally flooded streambeds). Overall, vegetated wetlands predominated, comprising 91 percent of the wetlands.

Estuarine Wetlands. Estuarine emergent wetlands alone made up 81 percent of the area's wetlands. Irregularly flooded wetlands (i.e., inundated less than daily by tides) represented 90 percent of the estuarine wetlands, with the rest being regularly flooded (i.e., subject to daily flooding). Common reed dominated or co-dominated nearly 97 percent of the estuarine wetlands. According to the updated NWI maps, slightly brackish wetlands were more abundant than the more saline types. The former type accounted for 2,871.3 acres or 59 percent of the estuarine wetlands. Nonvegetated wetlands (mostly regularly flooded tidal flats) represented about eight percent of the estuarine wetlands.

Palustrine Wetlands. Emergent wetlands also dominated the freshwater reaches of the Meadowlands area. They represented almost 48 percent of the palustrine wetlands and 58 percent of the vegetated types. Common reed marshes were most abundant. This species dominated or co-dominated 41 percent of the palustrine wetlands. It produced significant cover for 72 percent of the palustrine emergent wetlands (including mixed communities with shrubs). Forested wetlands covered nearly 200 acres, counting mixed shrub/forested types. Two-thirds of the forested wetlands were nontidal, while one third was tidal.

Deepwater Habitats

Ninety-eight percent of the area's deepwater habitats was estuarine (salt/brackish) water (4,264.5 acres). The remaining deepwater habitat was represented by 39.1 acres of lacustrine waters and 32.4 acres of riverine waters (mostly tidal fresh).

Figure 3. Map showing the general distribution of wetlands and deepwater habitats in the Hackensack Meadowlands area in 1995 based on the National Wetlands Inventory.

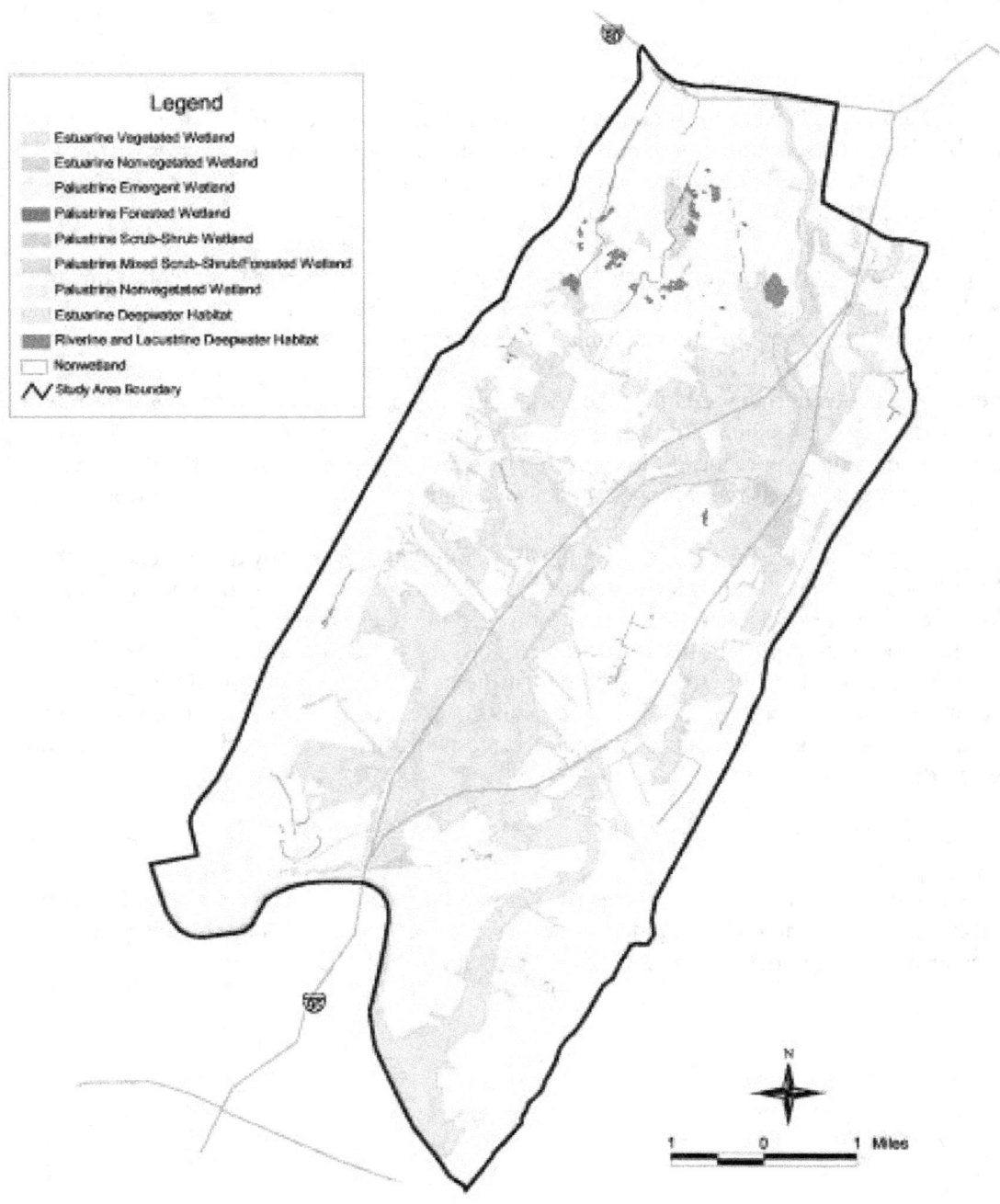

Table 10. Status of wetlands in the Meadowlands region in 1995.

Wetland Type	Acreage
Estuarine Wetlands	
Aquatic Bed Regularly Flooded	1.0
Emergent Irregularly Flooded	4,360.2
	(includes 4,236.7 a. w/Phragmites)
Emergent Regularly Flooded	103.8 (includes 87.0 a. w/Phragmites)
Scrub-Shrub Irregularly Flooded	13.0
Emergent/Scrub-Shrub Irregularly Flooded	12.2 (all w/Phragmites)
Scrub-Shrub/Emergent Irregularly Flooded	2.3 (all w/Phragmites)
Subtotal Estuarine Vegetated	4,492.5
Unconsolidated Shore Regularly Flooded	395.9
Unconsolidated Shore Irregularly Flooded	3.4
Subtotal Estuarine Nonvegetated	399.3
Total Estuarine	4,891.8
Palustrine Wetlands	
Emergent Tidal	181.9 (includes 164.6 a. w/Phragmites)
Emergent Nontidal	96.8 (includes 27.0 a. w/Phragmites)
Scrub-Shrub Tidal	17.2
Scrub-Shrub Nontidal	13.6
Emergent/Scrub-Shrub Tidal	28.0 (all w/Phragmites)
Forested Tidal	47.1
Forested Nontidal	63.0
Scrub-Shrub/Forested Tidal	16.1
Scrub-Shrub/Forested Nontidal	66.7
Subtotal Palustrine Vegetated	530.4
Unconsolidated Bottom Tidal	34.5
Unconsolidated Bottom Nontidal	54.0
Unconsolidated Shore Tidal	23.1
Subtotal Palustrine Nonvegetated	111.6
Total Palustrine	642.0
Riverine Wetlands	7.5
GRAND TOTAL – ALL WETLANDS	5,541.3

A Century of Aquatic Habitat Changes in the Meadowlands

A series of maps show the changes in wetlands from 1889 to 1995 (Figure 4 - map panel). The first map shows the approximate extent of wetlands in the study area in the late 1800s based on our interpretation of an 1889 topographic map compiled by the State of New Jersey. From this assessment, the study area had 20,045 acres of wetland and 2,943 acres of deepwater habitat in 1889. The other maps in Figure 4 show the distribution of wetlands on a decade basis from the 1950s to the 1990s. Through viewing these maps, one can see that the bulk of wetland changes took place between 1953/54 and 1984/85, with the greatest loss occurring from 1966-1976. The lower part of the Meadowlands (at the confluence of the Hackensack and Passaic Rivers) was destroyed prior to 1953/54. Table 11 summarizes the changes in the extent of wetlands and deepwater habitats from 1889 to 1995. During this 106-year period, wetlands dropped to slightly more than one quarter of their 1889 extent, while deepwater habitats increased by nearly 50 percent. Annual losses of wetland were calculated for the various intervals, with the results presented in Table 12. According to these figures, the greatest wetland losses took place from 1966 to 1976, with over 300 acres of wetland lost annually.

Table 11. Changes in the extent of wetlands and deepwater habitats in the Meadowlands area from 1889 to 1995.

Year	Wetland Acreage	% of 1889 Wetld Acreage	Deepwater Habitat (DWH) Acreage	% of 1889 DWH Acreage
1889	20,045	100%	2,943	100%
1953/54	13,419	67%	2,847	97%
1966	10,650	53%	3,855	131%
1976	7,607	38%	2,624	89%
1984/85	5,739	29%	4,321	147%
1995	5,541	28%	4,336	147%

Table 12. Annual wetland loss rates for the Meadowlands area.

Time Period	Total Wetland Acreage Lost	Annual Wetland Loss Rate (acres/yr)
1889-1953/54	6,626	102
1953/54-1966	2,769	231
1966-1976	3,043	304
1976-1984/85	1,868	208
1984/85-1995	198	20

Figure 4. Sequence of maps showing the general extent of wetland, water, and dryland (upland) in the Meadowlands study area from 1889 to 1995.

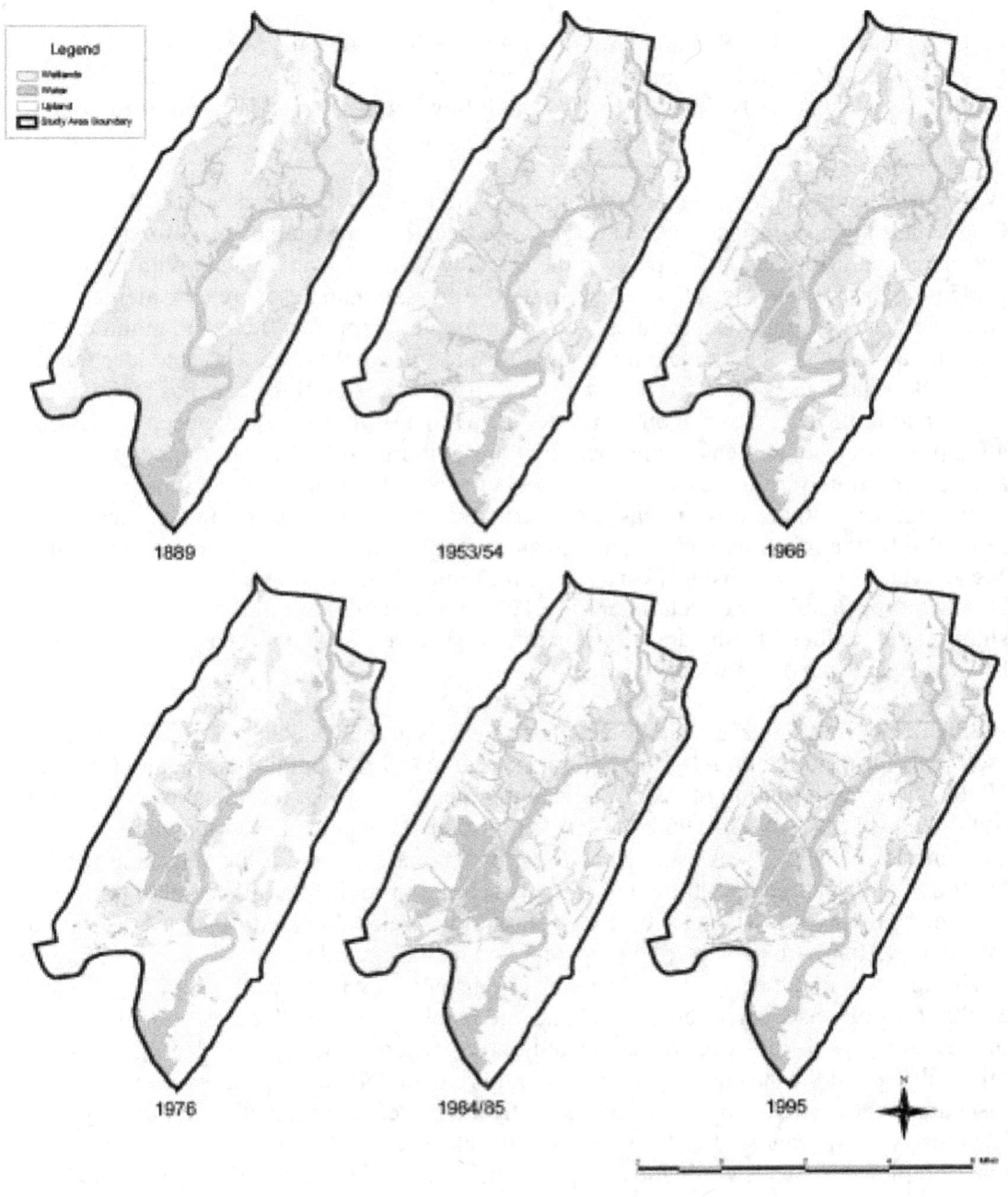

Discussion

John Quinn's "Fields of Sun and Grass: An Artist's Journal of the New Jersey Meadowlands" (Quinn 1997) presents a descriptive account of how the Meadowlands have changed since early times. Much of the following discussion is taken from this book.

While the Meadowlands were used by native Americans to hunt game and gather other foods, their most significant impact might have been burning marshes and forests to flush out the game. More lasting impacts to the Meadowlands probably began with European settlement of the New York City area. In the 1700s, salt marshes were considered valuable property, and local statutes were promulgated to protect them and maintain them for salt hay harvest. There were many uses for the salt hay besides winter fodder for livestock. These uses included roof thatching, packing material for bananas and glass, paper, and improving traction on winter roads. Dutch settlers may have been the first to attempt to drain some areas to improve their agricultural use. Major drainage projects and construction of railroads greatly impacted the Meadowlands in the 1800s. As the population grew, there was increased concern about the abundance of mosquitoes produced by the Meadowlands. With advances in ditching technology in the 1900s, the Meadowlands were extensively ditched for mosquito control as well as to make the "land" more suitable for development. In 1922, construction of Oradell Reservoir significantly reduced freshwater flowage into the Hackensack River, changing the river's hydrology and salt-fresh water balance.

Filling of tidal wetlands and shallow aquatic habitats at the Hackensack River's mouth took place prior to the mid-1950s (Figure 4). Quinn (1997) contains an illustration of a 1930s photograph showing tons of garbage dumped in the "Newark meadows" just south of the Pulaski Skyway. In 1968, the Hackensack Meadowlands Development Commission (HMDC) was established to prepare a master plan for the "Hackensack Meadowlands District." Although originally set up to provide an orderly plan for reclaiming the Meadowlands (i.e., converting it to developable land), the HMDC would eventually attempt to promote development and manage solid waste, while protecting the environment.[3] In the early 1970s, wetlands in the Meadowlands were being filled with 30,000 tons of waste per week (Robichaud and Buell 1973). At this time, about one-third of New Jersey's solid waste was deposited in the Meadowlands (Quinn 1997). This and other filling and the succeeding industrial and urban development (e.g., wastewater discharges) have greatly impacted and significantly altered the quantity and quality of Meadowlands wetlands. The New Jersey Turnpike section through the Meadowlands was completed in 1971, while most of the landfills were closed in 1979 (Quinn 1997).

---

[3] The HMDC's name was officially changed to the New Jersey Meadowlands Commission in August 2001 (http://www.hmdc.state.nj.us).

By 1995, only 28 percent of the wetlands that occurred in the late 19th Century remained, and most were severely degraded. The HMDC (now the New Jersey Meadowlands Commission) has set aside more than 8,400 acres for open space, waterways, and wetlands (Figure 5). Only one third of the wetlands in the District occurs within the "Marshland Preservation Zone." Most wetlands within the designated Hackensack Meadowlands District are located in areas zoned for development and may be considered at risk (Figure 6; Table 13).

Despite the degradation and destruction of habitat, the Meadowlands remain a viable fish and wildlife resource. More than 265 species of birds use the area, including numerous breeding species of concern, such as black-crowned night heron (Nycticorax nycticorax), blue-winged teal (Anas discors), northern harrier (Circus cyaneus), common moorhen (Gallinula chloropus), American coot (Fulica americana), and spotted sandpiper (Actitis macularia) (U.S. Fish and Wildlife Service, et al. 2000). The Meadowlands is recognized as a major link along the Atlantic Flyway for migratory species (especially shorebirds) and an important overwintering area for species including canvasback (Aythya valisineria), redhead (Aythya americana), bufflehead (Bucephala albeola), lesser scaup (Aythya affinis), greater scaup (Aythya marila), ruddy duck (Oxyura jamaicensis), hooded merganser (Lophodytes cucullatus), and common merganser (Mergus merganser). It also serves as an important food source for the detritus-based food web of the New York/New Jersey Harbor Estuary ecosystem (U.S. Fish and Wildlife Service, et al. 2000). This urban wetland complex also provides significant natural aesthetics to the surrounding built-up landscape and offers opportunities to millions of people in the New York-Newark metropolitan area to see waterfowl (ducks, Canada geese - Branta canadensis, common moorhen, and American coot), wading birds (herons, egrets, glossy ibis - Plegadis falcinellus, and occasionally the secretive least bittern - Ixobrychus exilis), shorebirds, numerous passerines (especially red-winged blackbird - Agelaius phoeniceus), muskrats (Ondatra zibethicus), raccoons (Procyon lotor), and other wildlife.

The future of the Meadowlands remains in the hands of New Jersey citizens, their public servants, and elected officials. Since the 1980s, the status of wetlands has improved with increased government protection, restoration initiatives, and the support of a more environmentally aware and concerned public. Yet, despite these gains, the Meadowlands will likely remain a threatened urban wildland due to its location and continued population and economic growth.

Figure 5. Map showing preservation areas, parks, and recreation areas in the Hackensack Meadowlands District. (Source: http://www.hmdc.state.nj.us)

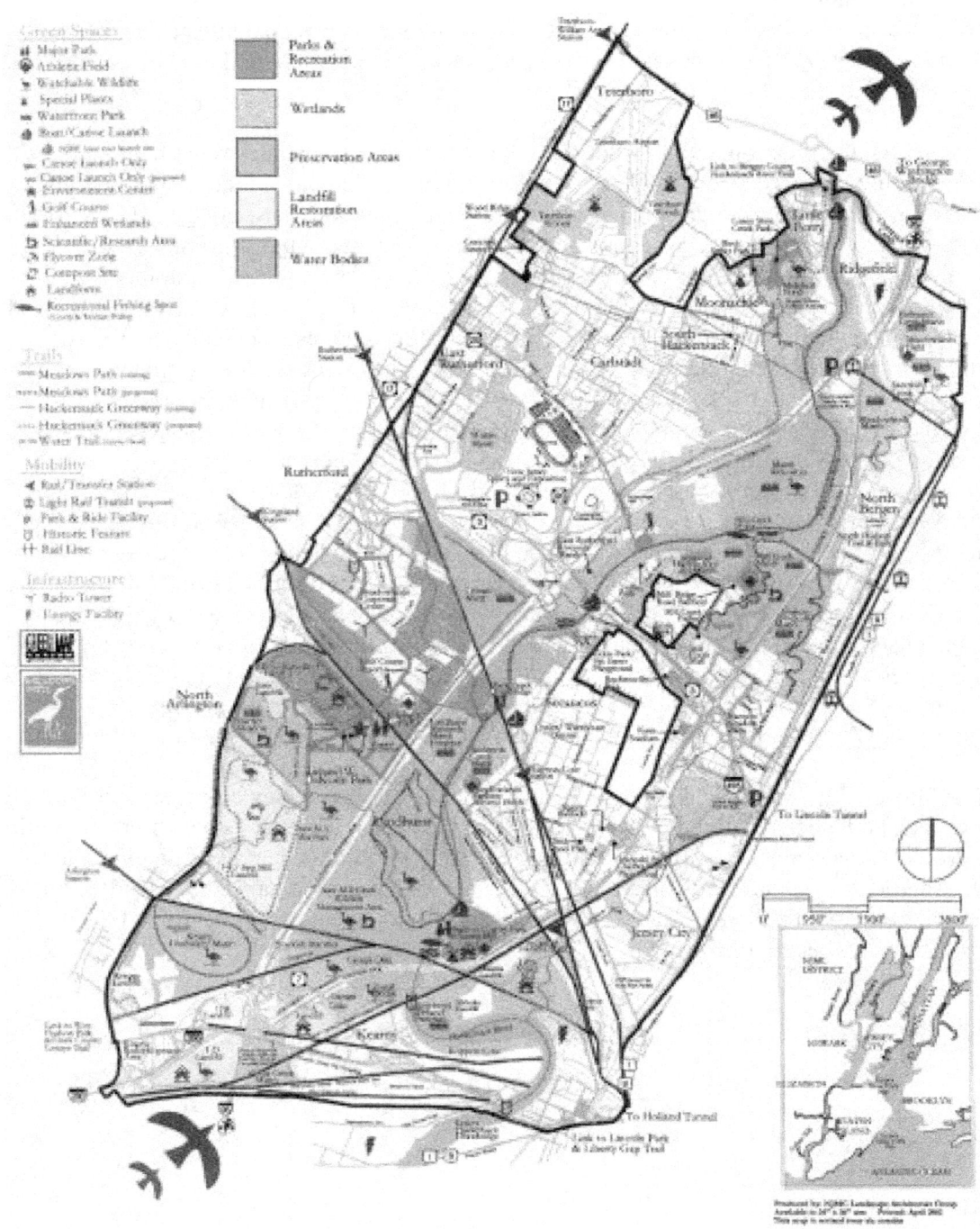

Figure 6. Map showing zoning for the Hackensack Meadowlands District. (Source: http://www.hmdc.state.nj.us)

Table 13. Extent of wetlands (including ponds) in designated zones within the Hackensack Meadowlands District. (<u>Note</u>: Our study area covers more area than this District.)

Zone	Acres of Estuarine Wetlands	Acres of Palustrine Wetlands	Total Wetland Acres
Airport Facilities	0	186.5	186.5
Berry's Creek Center	49.2	0	49.2
Commercial Park	0.6	0	0.6
Heavy Industrial	136.8	45.2	182.0
Highway Commercial	32.5	0	32.5
Island Residential	23.9	0	23.9
Light Industrial/Distr. A	371.9	27.5	399.4
Light Industrial/Distr. B	201.4	43.2	244.6
Limited Commercial	33.9	0	33.9
Low Density Residential	19.2	<0.1	19.2
Marshland Preservation	1,623.5	2.9	1,626.4
Park & Recreation	110.6	67.5	178.1
Parkside Residential 2	28.8	0	28.8
Parkside Residential 3	3.4	0	3.4
Planned Development Ctr	475.1	0	475.1
Public Utilities	110.6	2.6	113.2
Redevelopment Area	431.2	39.7	470.9
Research Distribution Park	87.7	0	87.7
Research Park	0.4	0	0.4
Service Highway Commer.	2.9	0	2.9
Special Use 1	36.6	0	36.6
Special Use 2	152.1	0	152.1
Special Use 3	148.7	1.6	150.3
Sports Complex	140.1	25.0	165.1
Transportation Center 1	0	31.3	31.3
Transportation Center 3	11.9	0	11.9
Water	186.8	0.6	187.4
Waterfront Recreation	11.8	3.5	15.3
Wetlands Totals	*4,431.6*	*477.1*	*4,908.7*

The U.S. Fish and Wildlife Service (Service) and the New Jersey Division of Fish and Wildlife (NJDFW) have established the following goals for the Meadowlands (U.S. Fish and Wildlife Service 2002):

- Improve conditions for all native plant, fish and wildlife species
- Clean up contaminated sites and reduce the effects of pollution on fish and wildlife
- Acquire, preserve, and restore remaining undeveloped tracts of land to key functioning parts of the Meadowlands ecosystem
- Control invasive and exotic species
- Enhance, restore, and maintain ecosystem integrity
- Increase public awareness and education about the Meadowlands and its regional importance through an expanded number of public access points with the Meadowlands, and by encouraging increased but ecologically responsible use of these public access facilities

The New Jersey Meadowlands Commission (NJMC) is acquiring wetlands and management rights and making zoning changes (e.g., redevelopment zones to Marshland Preservation Zone) in an effort to protect the remaining wetlands. Plans are also underway to restore the Hackensack Meadowlands ecosystem. The U.S. Army Corps of Engineers, the Service, and the NJMC are working on a feasibility study that will provide the foundation toward the development of a comprehensive restoration implementation plan. Wetland restoration and enhancement efforts include restoring tidal flow, removing contaminated soils, creating open water areas, controlling invasive species (common reed – Phragmites australis and purple loosestrife - Lythrum salicaria), and regulating water levels (www.meadowlands.state.nj.us/eip/wetlands.html). Presently, the NJMC is implementing these types of activities on 12 sites in the Meadowlands, while the NJDFW manages the Sawmill Creek Wildlife Management Area.

The main hope for the future of Meadowlands wetlands as well as for other urban wetlands is that as many as possible will be set aside as open space for our benefit and for future generations and that wetland restoration efforts will be accelerated to revitalize significantly impacted wetlands and to rebuild lost wetlands wherever practicable. Wetlands are natural resources that, among other things, increase the quality of life for urban residents across America.

Acknowledgments

Special thanks go to Dr. Benjamin Tuggle for providing support for this study. Ralph Tiner served as principal investigator for this project. He designed the study, analyzed the data, and prepared the report.

Technical support for this project was provided by Region 5 National Wetlands Inventory staff. John Swords performed wetland photointerpretation for the trends analysis, while interpretation of the 1995 photos to prepare updated NWI data was done by Lisa Reisner, Lauren McCubbin, and Meaghan Shaffer. Bobbi Jo McClain applied geographic information system (GIS) technology to prepare statistical summaries and maps/figures for the report. Herbert Bergquist and Gabriel DeAlessio assisted with GIS applications.

Staff from the Service's National Wetlands Inventory Center in St. Petersburg, Florida also contributed to the study. Of special note is Becky Stanley who did photo searches, ordered aerial photographs, and prepared work materials. She also located the 1889 topographic map that helped provide a historical perspective of our study's findings.

The Service's New Jersey Field Office provided some background material used for this report and reviewed the draft report.

References

Cowardin, L.M., V. Carter, F.C. Golet, and E.T. LaRoe. 1979. Classification of Wetlands and Deepwater Habitats of the United States. U.S. Fish and Wildlife Service, Washington, DC. FWS/OBS-79/31.

Quinn, J.R. 1997. Fields of Sun and Grass: An Artist's Journal of the New Jersey Meadowlands. Rutgers University Press, New Brunswick, NJ.

Robichaud, B. and M. F. Buell. 1973. Vegetation of New Jersey. Rutgers University Press, New Brunswick, NJ.

U.S. Fish and Wildlife Service. 2002. Field Notes, December 2002 - The Hackensack Meadowlands issue. New Jersey Field Office, Pleasantville, NJ.

U.S. Fish and Wildlife Service. 1996. Significant Habitats and Habitat Complexes of the New York Bight Watershed. U.S. Department of the Interior, Fish and Wildlife Service, Southern New England-New York Bight Coastal Ecosystems Program, Charlestown, RI.

U.S. Fish and Wildlife Service, U.S. Army Corps of Engineers, U.S. Environmental Protection Agency, National Marine Fisheries Service, and Hackensack Meadowlands Development Commission. 2000. Wildlife Management Plan for the Hackensack Meadowlands. Interagency report coordinated by the U.S. Fish and Wildlife Service, New Jersey Field Office, Pleasantville, NJ.

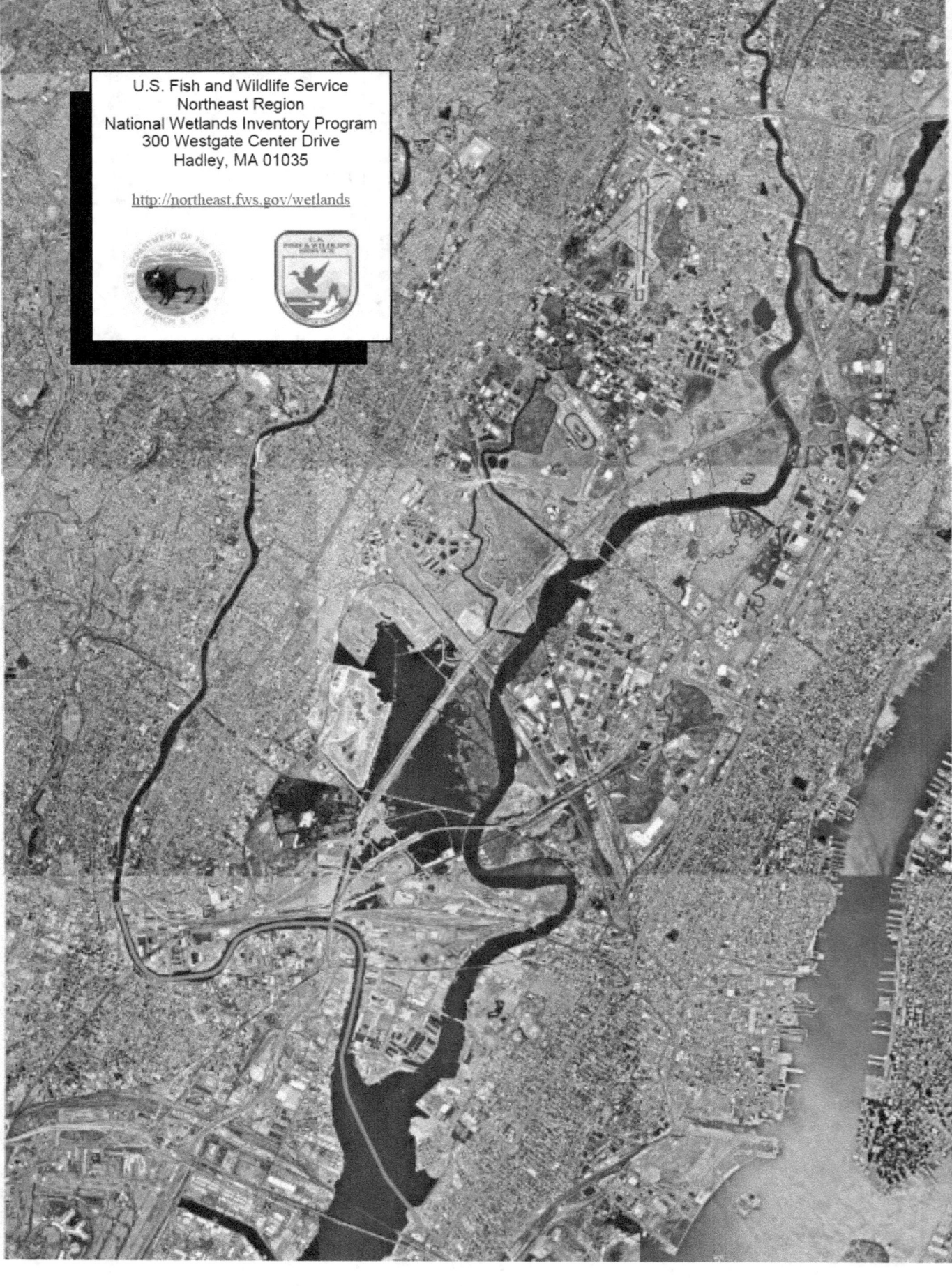

U.S. Fish and Wildlife Service
Northeast Region
National Wetlands Inventory Program
300 Westgate Center Drive
Hadley, MA 01035

http://northeast.fws.gov/wetlands

www.ingramcontent.com/pod-product-compliance
Lightning Source LLC
Chambersburg PA
CBHW081137280526
45787CB00007B/3126